God Speaks

GWENDOLYN McDOWELL

authorHOUSE®

AuthorHouse™
1663 Liberty Drive
Bloomington, IN 47403
www.authorhouse.com
Phone: 1-800-839-8640

© 2012 Gwendolyn McDowell. All rights reserved.

No part of this book may be reproduced, stored in a retrieval system, or transmitted by any means without the written permission of the author.

Published by AuthorHouse   11/28/2012

ISBN: 978-1-4772-6825-4 (sc)
ISBN: 978-1-4772-6826-1 (hc)
ISBN: 978-1-4772-6824-7 (e)

Any people depicted in stock imagery provided by Thinkstock are models, and such images are being used for illustrative purposes only.
Certain stock imagery © Thinkstock.

Because of the dynamic nature of the Internet, any web addresses or links contained in this book may have changed since publication and may no longer be valid. The views expressed in this work are solely those of the author and do not necessarily reflect the views of the publisher, and the publisher hereby disclaims any responsibility for them.

Foreword

You know what? You are not the problem. So, stop getting upset. Don't listen to the lies of the devil. You shine so brightly that darkness cannot stand you! That's why they call you names like "self-righteous" and say, "You think you're all that." What they see in you is the way they ought to be living. Do not fret. Do not run; just stand. Keep being holy and walk in love. Be courageous and strong. The Holy Spirit is a gentleman who doesn't force anyone to do anything. Unforgiveness, strife, hatred—leave it all alone. Don't stop loving. Don't stop being kind. Every time the devil sees you walking in love, he gets angry because you are exemplifying Christ. Some brothers and sisters in the body of Christ are frustrated with themselves, but they don't want you to know that, nor do they want to work to be delivered. They take it out on you because you are living a victorious life. But guess what, if they tapped into the Word of God like you do, they could live a victorious life in Jesus too. Let us pray that the eyes of their understanding be enlightened.

Table of Contents

WITNESS	XII
Go, Young People, Go!	1
God's Promises	3
Cowards in the Valley	5
SALVATION	6
I Did It Because I Love You	7
It Doesn't Matter	9
GOD IS IN CONTROL	10
You Don't Need to Know Everything	11
TRUST IN THE LORD	12
Trust in God Alone	13
Them or Jesus	15
LOVE YOUR ENEMIES	16
To My Enemies	17
EXAMINE YOURSELF	18
No Matter What	19
KEEP IT MOVING	20
Forget and Press Forward	21
Getting Over It	23
OUR ENEMY	24
Thank God for Jesus	25
I Found You Out, Satan!	27
PASTORS	28
A Talk with God about Pastor	29
We Love You, Pastor	31

Happy Birthday, Pastor!	33
ANGELS	**36**
God's Angels	37
Angels Talking	39
SIN	**40**
It Happens	41
Reflect and Don't Forget	43
Go Away!	45
Be Done!	47
It's Rhema to Me Now!	49
TEMPTATION	**52**
Temptation	53
Wait on the Lord	55
Slow Down	57
TESTS AND TRIALS	**58**
Tests	59
FLESH V SPIRIT	**60**
Let's Do This	61
WATCH YOUR MOUTH!	**62**
Gossip in the Church	63
Hallelujah!	65
GOD WILL PROVIDE	**66**
Jars of Oil, Flour in the Bin	67
ARE YOU READY?	**68**
I'm Coming Soon	69
WORTHY	**70**
His	71
THE CHOICE IS YOURS	**72**

My Choice	73
CREATION, THE FALL OF MAN, AND REDEMPTION	**74**
How Did This Happen?	75
CHILDREN OF GOD	**80**
My Children	81
HUSBAND & WIFE	**82**
I Love You	83
DYING TO SELF	**84**
Self and Jesus	85
TITHING	**88**
Saints Tithe!	89
About the Author	91
About the Book	93

WITNESS

But ye shall receive power, after that the Holy Ghost is come upon you: and ye shall be witnesses unto Me both in Jerusalem, and in all Judea, and in Samaria, and unto the uttermost part of the earth.

—Acts 1:8 KJV

Go, Young People, Go!

Young people, surely there's no doubt
That all of you must go out.

Go get my people; they are lost.
Please be willing to pay the cost.

Plenty of seats on each bus;
Get on board, don't make a fuss.

Don't ask yourself, "What will I say?"
Tell them I'm the only way.

They will confess Me with their mouth.
Go, young people, north, east, west, and south.

Go spread My name and you will see:
Yes, all those souls belong to Me.

I've told you once, I'll tell you again:
Go get my people and bring them in.

God's Promises

Unity and bonds of love rest on each of you.

Disobedience is bound, and gossipers are through.

A new beginning—walk ye in, forgetting the past.

Restoration for all; you are restored at last.

I've healed you in your spirit, your body, and your soul.

I've strengthened each of you so you can reach your blessed goal.

Entire families are saved—rejoice and be at peace.

Your father, mother, and aunts are saved, your nephews and your niece.

Cities have I given you; you are all millionaires.

Preach the gospel, take the land, and possess, for you are heirs.

Gather all the people. Thousands will go out—

As the thousands enter in, rejoice with a shout!

Bear witness to the prostitutes, the rich, and the poor.
You are prepared for the many thousands at the door.

Governments and leaders will repent of their sin.
Turning from their wicked ways, I will enter in.

Everywhere your feet will touch, the land is surely yours,
So make a stand. I love you all, my mighty warriors.

Cowards in the Valley

Cowards in the valley of decision to go out:
So many souls to witness. They're wandering about.

Cowards in the valley, afraid to take the land.
Cowards in the valley, reach out and take My hand.

Cowards in the valley, please join the others now.
You must be brave, no more fear, no more questions how.

Cowards in the valley, I will tell you what to say.
Be not afraid. Will you go out? Will you go out today?

Cowards in the valley, by faith is how it's done.
Fear has overtaken you, causing you to run.

Cowards, in the valley is not the place to be;
I need you as My instruments, to set the captives free.

Cowards in the valley, put your trust in Me.
I have never let you down, you know you must agree.

Coward in the valley, a soldier, will you be?
Then be a soldier in My army—go witnessing for Me!

Salvation

For God so loved the world, that He gave His only begotten Son, that whosoever believeth in Him, should not perish, but have everlasting life.

—John 3:16 KJV

And the Word was made flesh, and dwelt among us (and we beheld His glory, the glory as of the only begotten of the Father,) full of grace and truth.

—John 1:14 KJV

I Did It Because I Love You

On your behalf, I became flesh and dwelt among you all;
The only way for man to be redeemed from Adam's fall.

I came prepared, and yes, I was the perfect sacrifice.
You were purchased with My blood, brought with a price.

I died for you; I rose for you, all power in My hand;
Now live abundantly, enjoy and prosper in this land.

Health divine is yours because My stripes of thirty-nine
Bear your sicknesses; no longer yours, because they're Mine.

Instead of you, I went to hell and snatched the devil's keys
From hell and death I snatched them both and knocked him to his knees!

A spectacle I made of him; he's underneath your feet.
He's quite aware the victory's yours and he is in defeat.

It's finished, done, the cross completed back at Calvary;
Done because of love and done so you will reign with Me.

It Doesn't Matter

It doesn't matter what this world may think about you anymore.

The only thing that matters is I died so you might live.

No matter what the world may say,

No matter what may come your way,

No matter; trust in Me alone.

No matter what, this is not your home.

It doesn't matter what this world may think about you anymore.

The only thing that matter is I died so you might live.

God Is in Control

For My thoughts are not your thoughts, neither are your ways My ways, saith the Lord. For as the heavens are higher than the earth, so are My ways higher than your ways, and My thoughts than your thoughts.

—Isaiah 55:8–9 KJV

You Don't Need to Know Everything

Stop trying to figure out what God is gonna do.

All you need to know is that it's working out for you.

Don't you trust in the Lord with all of your heart?

Leave God alone, please; let go, don't pick his brain apart!

He'll tell you what you need to know.

This, in turn will help you grow.

Trust in the Lord

Trust in the Lord with all thine heart; and lean not unto thine own understanding. In all thy ways acknowledge Him, and He shall direct thy paths.

—Proverbs 3:5–6 KJV

Trust in God Alone

Sometimes you love, and hate is returned.

When will we ever learn?

To put our trust in no man

To trust in God's unchanging hand

He is love and love alone;

To every creature this love is shown.

THEM OR JESUS

I can't worry what others say;
They'll talk about me anyway.

I simply cannot please everyone;
Only Jesus Christ, God's Son.

I have to stand for what is right.
God will take me to higher heights.

The Lord will take care of all the others,
For they are all my sisters and brothers.

He'll talk to all of them about me.
Most likely they will bow their knees,

Repenting for all the things they said.
Forgiving each other, we'll press ahead.

Love Your Enemies

But I say unto you, Love your enemies, bless them that curse you, do good to them that hate you, and pray for them which despitefully use and persecute you.

—Matthew 5:44 KJV

For if ye love them which love you, what reward have ye?

—Matthew 5:46 KJV

To My Enemies

I heap coals of fire upon the heads that do me in

By showing love to them, although they're really not my friends.

If they hunger, I will feed them to their hearts' content.

Maybe this act of love will cause them to repent.

If they thirst, the Bible tells me, give them a drink.

I pray showing God's love to them will make them stop and think.

I won't respond to the evil things they've done to me;

I'll love them from my heart, without hypocrisy.

I'll be kind, affectionate, and bless them when I pray.

Although they persecute my soul, I'll bless them anyway.

I pray showing God's love to them will cause their schemes to cease.

Help me, God, to love them; let my love for them increase.

With You, oh Lord, it's possible—Your Word so does confirm—

To love my enemies, expecting nothing in return.

Examine Yourself

But be ye doers of the Word, and not hearers only, deceiving your own selves. For if any be a hearer of the Word, and not a doer, he is like unto a man beholding his natural face in a glass: For he beholdeth himself, and goeth his way, and straightway forgetteth what manner of man he was. But whoso looketh into the perfect law of liberty, and continueth therein, he being not a forgetful hearer but a doer of the work, this man shall be blessed in his deed.

—James 1:22–25 KJV

No Matter What

No matter what you did to me, I did not do what is right.
I blame myself for falling short, not walking in God's light.

No matter what you did to me, I should have shown you love.
My tongue got me in trouble with our Father up above.

No matter what you did to me, I'm the one to blame.
I was warned, my guard let down, now I am ashamed.

No matter what you did to me, I can only look at me.
My actions, yes, they were in flesh, ungodly as can be.

No matter what you did to me, I reconcile with you.
I will love you anyway, no matter what you do.

Keep It Moving

Brethren, I count not myself to have apprehended: but this one thing I do, forgetting those things which are behind, and reaching forth unto those things which are before, I press toward the mark for the prize of the high calling of God in Christ Jesus.

—Philippians 3:13–14 KJV

Forget and Press Forward

In the past my heart was full of judging and complaints.

It's Rhema now that each and every one of you are saints.

I'm learning more and more to love you just like Jesus does.

He loves us unconditionally; He loves us just because.

All I see is Christ in you—that's all I want to see—

No more faults, no more flaws. I love you unconditionally.

Getting Over It

Many times I have been burned;
So many lessons have I learned

From those I loved and drew so close.
They all gave me a double dose:

Resentment, hate, and anger too.
Don't feel sad; this is not new.

Growing from it bit by bit,
I have gotten over it.

It won't forever be this way;
Jesus is coming back one day

To take all of my tears away.
There will be nothing they can say,

For I'll be lying in Jesus' arms.
Yes, they'll regret they did me harm.

Our Enemy

Put on the whole armor of God, that ye may be able to stand against the wiles of the devil. For we wrestle not against flesh and blood, but against principalities, against powers, against the rulers of the darkness of this world, against spiritual wickedness in high places.

—Ephesians 6:11–12 KJV

Behold, I give unto you power to tread on serpents and scorpions, and over all the power of the enemy: and nothing shall by any means hurt you.

—Luke 10:19 KJV

Thank God for Jesus

Satan's doing all he can,
But never will he destroy God's plan!

Picking and plucking at us saints,
Accusing us, with all kinds of complaints,

Watching and waiting to do us in,
Still he's defeated—he'll never win!

He's always trying to make us fall,
but we won't give in to him at all.

Satan's always on our trail.
We slip and fall and sometimes fail.

Sin at first seems so nice,
But in the end, is a horrible price.

But that's okay, for Jesus died.
No need to worry; He's on our side.

Our sins He bore on Calvary
That we may live eternally.

I Found You Out, Satan!

I know your games, I know your ways, I know the lies you tell.
I will not be deceived anymore; I will not go to hell.

You thought I'd never find out all the tricks and games you play,
But you should know by now, it is the Lord I obey.

I do not care what threats you make; I'm covered by God's blood.
The only thing I see you covered by is piles of mud.

You had the nerve to steal the blessing my God gave to me.
Guess what, you thief! I found out that I have authority!!

Thank God for angelology and demonology;
My pastor taught me all I need to know to make you flee.

I know now, I have power over all you do and say.
That's right; I know there's nothing you can do to make me stray.

Give up! Get lost! Get out! Be gone, in Jesus' name, I pray.
I know when you're rebuked in Jesus' name you'll go away!

Pastors

And I will give you pastors according to mine heart, which shall feed you with knowledge and understanding.

—Jeremiah 3:15 KJV

A Talk with God about Pastor

Me: Pastor sure can teach!
He's humble and he's meek.

God: He's anointed from on high;
This is the reason why.

Me: I thank you, Lord and Master,
For my beloved Pastor.

God: Cherish him, indeed.
Learn and follow as he leads.

Me: Learn and follow—yes, I will!
His love for You is very real.

God: Yes, he's faithful and he's just.
Your Pastor you can trust.

We Love You, Pastor

We thank God for your preaching
Because it keeps us reaching.

We thank God for your teaching
Because it keeps us seeking.

We thank God for your praying;
It keeps us all from straying.

We thank God for your stand;
We trust in God, not man.

We thank God for your cost;
You've reached out to the lost.

We thank God for your time;
You'd never charge a dime.

We thank God for your faith,
For truly it is great.

We thank our God for you;
We're blessed for all you do.

Happy Birthday, Pastor!

Run, leap, jump, and shout!
Saints of God, dance about!

Pastor's birthday is today!
Celebrate and shout hooray!

Clap your hands and nod your head
In the Spirit as you are led;

Wave your hands and raise them high!
You can do it, don't be shy!

It ain't nothing but the truth:
Jesus has renewed his youth.

Strong in Spirit, in health, divine,
Full of life tapped in the vine.

You see, his eyesight is not dim,
So watch yourself, little Jim.

Young people of God say, "He's so cool,"
Never letting his flesh rule.

Like an eagle in the sky,
He soars through trials—what a guy!

Look at Pastor strike a pose
In his happy birthday clothes,

Praising God for another year,
Strong in Sprit, full of cheer.

"Bless the Lord, oh my soul,"
Is what he says to reach his goal.

With loving kindness he is crowned.
Amazing grace, how sweet the sound.

NGELS

For He shall give His angels charge over thee, to keep thee in all thy ways. They shall bear thee up in their hands, Lest thou dash thy foot against a stone.

—Psalms 91:11–12 KJV

Bless the Lord, ye His angels, that excel in strength, that do His commandments, hearkening unto the voice of His Word.

—Psalm 103:20 KJV

Praise ye Him, all His angels: Praise ye Him, all his host.

—Psalm 148:2 KJV

God's Angels

Seraphims are close to God. They are an awesome sight.
They are the burning ones of God; they're radiant and bright.

The cherubim: four wings they have, four faces so unique.
They guard the gates of Eden; we know they are not weak.

Thrones, we know, have fiery wheels. They too have many eyes.
They carry out decisions from our God, who's truly wise.

Dominions regulate their own. Their duties must be done:
These angels do their duty by giving praise to God's dear Son.

Fallen angels often try to run the human race,
But Powers are in charge, you see, to keep them in their place.

Evil angels try invasions of our government,
But it won't work; that is why Principalities are sent.

Archangels are most common. They communicate with you.
They bring the messages from God; we know their words are true.

Angels Talking

Why do you continue to go back?
Is there something that you lack?

Do you really enjoy this pain?
Is there something for you to gain?

You walk and groan with your head hung down.
No one else sees, but we're around.

We see your hurt, we see your sorrow.
You think, "No hope for me tomorrow."

You must know that Jesus is
All you want, for you are His.

Don't go back to places of dark;
Jesus wants all of your heart.

He wants you whole, to tell the story.
He wants to use you for His glory

Receive restoration in your life,
Freedom from misery and strife.

Sin

For the wages of sin is death; but the gift of God is eternal life through Jesus Christ our Lord.

—Romans 6:23 KJV

If we say we have no sin, we deceive ourselves, and the truth is not in us.

—1 John 1:8 KJV

And if any man sin, we have an advocate with the Father, Jesus Christ the righteous.

—1 John 2:1 KJV

It Happens

You wonder where your blessings went—
But have you been obedient?

God warned you, time and time again,
But you continued in your sin.

He told you to repent and pray;
You turned your back and went your way.

It wasn't 'til you fell, half-dead,
You turned to God and begged and begged!

"I humbly fall down on my knees!
Have mercy, Lord! Forgive me, please!"

God did just what He does the best:
Forgave your sins and gave you rest.

Now, wait on God and He'll restore.
Stay close to Him and sin no more.

Reflect and Don't Forget

We stood there thinking we were strong,
But found out we were very wrong.

Temptation came so quick and fast,
We thought that sin was in our past.

That sinful thought danced in our heads.
Satan pleased, had more ahead.

We should have prayed and rebuked him then;
Instead we entertained and sinned.

Off guard, we were not taking heed;
We slipped and fell, and sinned indeed.

Forgive us, God, we've sinned again.
We'll stay on guard; we will not sin.

Go Away!

Deliverance any day now from this sin that has me bound.

The thing I do is sickening, done when no one is around.

I know God sees me doing this—I do it anyway,

Giving in to Satan's tricks. Confess, repent, I pray!

I feel so bad and hurt inside that Jesus sees me bare.

However, I still feel His touch, His tender loving care.

Sometimes I feel I won't give in, but give in anyhow.

It's time to stop—this same old sin will stop right here and now!

I plead the blood of Jesus Christ against you, enemy.

You know your name—they're more than one—so get thee behind me!

BE DONE!

Be done with lust!
This is a must.

Be done with hate
And love your mate.

Be done with lies;
No more disguise.

Be done with strife;
You have new life.

Be done with doubt;
God's worked it out.

Be done with cares;
We all are heirs.

Be done with pride;
Let God abide.

It's Rhema to Me Now!

I never should have doubted you.
I was in sin, what could I do?

My life got worse every day.
Although I prayed, there was delay.

What was I doing oh so wrong?
My prayers went from short to long.

Before, I dwelt in places of dark.
The world almost tore me apart.

Before, I dwelt in ugly places,
Mingling with demonic faces.

Soon Rhema came shining through
To let me know just what to do.

My pastor said to keep God's Word.
Not doing that, I'm sure you've heard

My pastor preached on covenant—
I hadn't known what that meant.

He made so simple things in question,
Which led me to sincere confession.

Now I keep God's covenant.
Blessings received are heaven-sent.

Temptation

There hath no temptation taken you but such as is common to man: but God is faithful, who will not suffer you to be tempted above that you are able; but will with the temptation also make a way to escape, that ye may be able to bear it.

—1 Corinthians 10:13 KJV

Temptation

Lord, help me to endure temptation.
Deliver me from this one frustration.

I desire to do Your will,
But Satan's here to kill and steal.

I let my guard down way too much.
Remind me of Your holy touch.

Be on guard both day and night
So Satan has no chance to fight.

WAIT ON THE LORD

I waited and I waited,
So many times frustrated.

Anxious I became;
I murmured and complained.

I fasted and I prayed
For God to give me aid.

I said with many tears,
"I wonder if He hears."

Surely, day by day,
My burdens rolled away.

My tears no longer found,
My mind was calm and sound.

I waited for a while.
Delivered now, I smile.

Sometimes it's very hard,
I've learned, to wait on God.

Slow Down

Each day, I have to take it slow.
It's hard sometimes—I'm sure you know.

Trials and tribulations I face.
Thank God for His amazing grace.

His grace has not left me alone;
Because of this, I've truly grown.

I'm learning more and more to press
And not put up with Satan's mess.

I'm learning more and more to love
Like our dear Father up above.

Each day, I have to take it slow.
Please help me Lord, I want to grow.

Tests and Trials

Beloved, think it not strange concerning the fiery trial which is to try you, as though some strange thing happened unto you: But rejoice, inasmuch as ye are partakers of Christ's sufferings; that, when His glory shall be revealed, ye may be glad also with exceeding joy.

—1 Peter 4:12 KJV

TESTS

You must be tested and be tried

So you'll be cleansed and purified.

Tests will help you to endure

Your calling and election, sure.

Maturity and strength: you will gain both.

Yes, testing is a part of growth.

Tests will sometimes make you cry

But when it's over, what a sigh!

Another test is on the way.

Be ready any time of day.

Flesh v Spirit

For the Flesh Lusteth Against the Spirit, and the Spirit against the Flesh

This I say then, Walk in the Spirit, and ye shall not fulfill the lust of the flesh.

—Galatians 5:16 KJV

Let's Do This

Love	when there is hate.
Smile	when there is sadness.
Pray	when there is strife.
Unite	when there is division.
Reach out	when there is withdrawal.
Forgive	when there is unforgiveness.
Confess	when there is guilt.
Repent	when there is sin.
Hug	when there is pain.
Encourage	when there is discouragement.
Faith	when there is doubt.
Strengthen	when there is weakness.
Stand	when you fall.
Press on	when it gets tough (the tough gets going).
Joy	when there is sorrow.

Watch Your Mouth!

If any man among you seem to be religious, and bridleth not his tongue, but deceiveth his own heart, this man's religion is vain.

—James 1:26 KJV

Set a watch, O Lord, before my mouth; Keep the door of my lips.

—Psalm 141:3 KJV

Gossip in the Church

Your gossip causes so much strife;
It causes heartache in one's life.

One trusts in you to understand;
Instead, you run from man to man.

Just in case you're unaware,
The ones you tell—they do not care.

They only seek to destroy one's name
By bringing their lives to open shame.

You reveal one's life for all to see.
I just can't see how this could be.

A man was fighting with his spouse,
Because of your gossip, in God's house.

So many friendships you've destroyed;
You're now the one whom I avoid.

I pray your gossip will truly end.
You never know who you'll offend.

HALLELUJAH!

Hallelujah, because I cried unto You.

Hallelujah, because You brought me through.

Hallelujah, because You fixed it for me.

Hallelujah, because I know I'm free.

Hallelujah, because You're worthy to be praised.

Hallelujah, because I'm so amazed.

Hallelujah, because You're never too late.

Hallelujah, because You never make a mistake.

Hallelujah, because You suffered, bled and died.

Hallelujah, because in You, I'll always abide.

Hallelujah, I praise You without shame!

Hallelujah, and bless Your Holy name!

God Will Provide

But my God shall supply all your need according to His riches in glory by Christ Jesus.

—Philippians 4:19 KJV

Therefore I say unto you, take no thought for your life, what ye shall eat, or what ye shall drink; nor yet for your body, what ye shall put on. Is not the life more than meat, and the body than raiment?

—Matthew 6:25 KJV

Jars of Oil, Flour in the Bin

Your jars of oil will not run dry.
Pour on, My child. You will not die.

In days of famine, I'll have in store
More jars of oil for you to pour.

Pour on, My child, there's plenty of oil.
In famine days, you will not toil.

Worry not and do not fret;
I am the oil. There's better yet:

Flour, flour in your bin.
In famine days, you won't grow thin.

Elijah, widow, and son I fed
With oil and flour for their bread.

Your jars of oil will not run dry.
Pour on, My child. You will not die.

Are You Ready?

Behold, He cometh with clouds; and every eye shall see Him.

—Revelation 1:7 KJV

I'M COMING SOON

I'm coming back, coming soon.
Will you be ready, night or noon?

I'm in the clouds, I'm on My way;
Make preparations without delay.

Just keep on looking in the clouds,
Father, mother, brother, child.

Be all ye ready, the rapture's near.
Soon no more sorrow, for I'll be here.

I'm coming back, coming soon.
Will you be ready, night or noon?

I'm in the clouds, I'm on My way;
Make preparations without delay.

Worthy is the lamb that was slain to receive power, and riches, and wisdom and strength and honor, and glory and blessing.

—Revelation 5:12 KJV

HIS

His love is unconditional,
He's grace and even merciful

His mercy always will endure;
His promises are real and sure.

His power shows throughout the earth,
His might and strength are filled with worth.

His worthiness we do proclaim;
His praise is shouted without shame.

His peace is unexplainable.
His joy remains unspeakable.

His strength in battle defeats all wrongs;
His victory is praised in songs.

His loving kindness never ends;
His blood was shed for all our sins.

His Word has all authority.
His kingdom reigns eternally.

The Choice is Yours

Choose you this day whom you will serve.

—Joshua 24:15 KJV

My Choice

I choose you, Lord; take all my heart.
Nothing will tear our love apart.

I choose you, Lord, to do Your will.
I'll run no more; I'll just be still.

I choose you, Lord; you know what's best.
I realize now I made a mess.

I choose you, Lord. Forgive me, please.
I humbly fall down on my knees.

My spirit, soul, and body I give.
I choose you, Lord, I want to live.

Choose the Lord your God and serve Him, bless Him, without cease.
The blessings our God has in store will abundantly increase.

Creation, the Fall of Man, and Redemption

And God said, let Us make man in Our image, after Our likeness: and let them have dominion.

—Genesis 1:26 KJV

And the Lord God said unto the woman, what is this that thou hast done?

—Genesis 3:13 KJV

And unto Adam He said, because thou hast hearkened unto the voice of thy wife and hast eaten of the tree, of which I commanded thee, saying, thou shalt not eat of it: cursed is the ground for thy sake; in sorrow shalt thou eat of it all the days of thy life.

—Genesis 3:17 KJV

How Did This Happen?

In the beginning, created I
Man in My image, never to die.

Male and female created I
To be fruitful and to multiply.

We had fellowship every day;
We were close in every way.

Dominion I gave them over all
The earth they ruled, 'til Adam's fall.

Of good and evil was the tree
That separated man from Me.

I told them, "From this tree, don't eat."
They failed; the devil had them beat.

I warned them they would surely die,
Instead, they listened to a lie.

I cursed the serpent and the ground,
For man had sinned and they were bound.

The tree of life was still about,
So from the garden, I drove them out!

Man was cursed—what could they do?
They were lost, and sinful too.

I wrote My laws on tablets of stone.
But man had failed, who would atone?

Man sacrificed with many beasts
In rituals by earthly priests.

Man was living much in sin.
The law was strict and would not bend.

Those sacrifices covered sin,
But what would make them whole again?

So Gabriel was sent to earth
To tell dear Mary of My birth.

Mary dwelt in Galilee,
A city of Nazareth, you see.

"Hail, Mary! Highly favored one,
You will surely bear a son."

I was wrapped in swaddling clothes;
Mary covered My little toes.

She held Me close and kept me warm,
For I, the Lord, had just been born.

Joseph smiled and gave God praise.
He was simply so amazed!

King Herod wanted Me to die.
He sent the wise men to be his spy.

The wise men knew not Herod's scheme.
What King Herod did was mean.

Before them went the eastern star.
They journeyed on, not very far.

When they arrived, they worshipped Me.
Their gifts were precious as can be.

Gold, frankincense, and myrrh—
Oh, how beautiful they were.

King Herod never came to Me;
My Father let the wise men see.

He told them all not to go back,
For Herod wanted to attack.

The wise men went to Herod not,
For in a dream, they saw his plot.

They left Me and went on their way—
They could have stayed another day!

I'm at the door, I stand and knock.
Will you be one of my flock?

God Speaks

Confess Me with your mouth this day,
For I am Jesus, the only way.

Believe God raised Me from the dead,
And follow after Me instead.

The choice is yours. That's why I came:
To redeem mankind from sin and shame.

Open up your hearts this day.
Receive salvation, I humbly pray.

Children of God

Lo, children are an heritage of the Lord.

—Psalm 127:3 KJV

My Children

It's a blessing to raise such a child;
Sometimes rough, sometimes mild,

Sometimes good, sometimes bad,
Sometimes happy, sometimes sad.

A blessing to teach them the ways of God,
To be true and not a fraud.

Sometimes they listen, sometimes they fall,
But learn their lessons from them all.

My patience does sometimes grow thin;
I pray to God to step right in.

He does all things so very well,
He'll never let my children fail.

Husband & Wife

Marriage is honorable in all.

—Hebrews 13:4 KJV

I Love You

There is no shame in our dear love;
It came from Father God above.

He joined us both to do His will.
Our love is true and very real.

His will be done in you and me;
Yes, you and I are meant to be.

Through thick and thin, you've been my friend,
Supporting me until the end.

I need you now more than before;
You are the one whom I adore.

I almost lost you, but our God knew—
He opened my eyes and now I see you!

Dying To Self

He must increase, but I must decrease.

—John 3:30 KJV

Self and Jesus

Self wants to be known.
Self wants to be shown.

Self wants attention.
Self wants competition.

Self wants praise.
Self wants to amaze.

Self says, "I'm a star."
Jesus says, "You've gone too far."

Self says, "I'm it!"
Jesus says, "Quit!"

Self says, "I'm on the throne."
Jesus says, "God, alone."

Self says, "I have arrived!"
Jesus says, "You're not wise."

Self says, "I did it all."
Jesus says, "Without Me, you'll fall."

Self says, "Who are you?"
Jesus says, "You know who."

Self says, "I don't need you."
Jesus says, "Oh, yes, you do!"

Self says, "I don't need to know."
Jesus says, "Then to hell you'll go."

Self says, "Oh, no, not there!"
Jesus says, "Then beware."

Jesus says, "I'm the truth and the life."
Self says, "I know, you're right."

Jesus says, "I'm the bright morning star."
Self says, "I've truly gone too far."

Jesus says, "Come unto me."
Self says, "What will I see?"

Jesus says, "I, in you."
Self says, "What will this do?"

Jesus says, "It'll kill your "self."
Self says, "I'll have nothing left."

Jesus says, "Oh, yes, you will."
Self says, "Are you for real?"

Jesus says, "I'll fill you up."
Self says, "Hey, here's my cup!"

Jesus says, "Depend on Me."
Self says, "Will I still be worthy?"

Jesus says, "You were nothing before."
Self says, "I thought I was all that and more."

Jesus says, "You're nothing without Me."
Self says, "Oh, I see."

Jesus says, "Without Me, you are nothing."
Self says, "But with you, I'm something?"

Jesus says, "That's right, My friend."
Self says, "Hey, I'm in sin."

Jesus says, "I died for you."
Self says, "I know that's true."

Jesus says, "Confess and repent."
Self listened. He knew what this meant.

Jesus looked at Self with loving eyes.
Self gave up "Self," and Self died.

Tithing

Bring ye all the tithes into the storehouse, that there may be meat in mine house, and prove me now herewith, saith the Lord of hosts, if I will not open you the windows of heaven, and pour you out a blessing, that there shall not be room enough to receive it.

—Malachi 3:10 KJV

SAINTS TITHE!

Saints, pay your tithes and offerings. This is not a curse;
Blessings you'll receive from Me, so open up your purse.

Ten percent is required from the one who's chief.
That ten percent is holy—if you take it, you're a thief.

Turn to Malachi and read, in chapter three, verse eight;
It's simple and explained without confusion or debate.

I know that some of you may think that this is not a crime,
But refuse to pay your offerings, and you will do some time!

That time will be a big, fat hole inside your pocketbook,
Always to remind you of the money that you took.

It you tithe, that hole will close; a bigger purse you'll buy.
You'll see, you can't beat God's giving, no matter how hard you try.

About the Author

Gwendolyn McDowell was born and raised in Washington, DC. When she was a child, her foster parents noticed she was gifted in the arts. At the early age of nine, Gwen began singing in the church choir and participating in plays and talent shows, which she continued to do from elementary through junior high school. At fourteen, she was accepted into the Vocal Major Department of the Duke Ellington School of the Performing Arts in Washington, DC.

She graduated from Duke Ellington in 1984. Her musical theater career has afforded her the opportunity to travel across the United States and to countries all over the world, including Jamaica, England, and Russia. Over the years, she has performed with various gospel artists such as the Richard Smallwood Singers, Lynette Hawkins, Maurette Brown-Clark, and Lacresia Campbell, to name a few.

Gwen currently lives in Maryland, where she continues to serve the Lord with the talents and gifts with which He blessed her.

She has two daughters, Mycah McDowell and Cierra Jennings, a son-in-law, Claude Jennings Jr., and a grandson, Claude Jennings III.

About the Book

Throughout Gwen's career in music and theater, God breathed words of encouragement, peace, and love to her soul. She penned these words into poems and used them over the years not only to edify herself, but also to encourage others. This book is a compilation of those poems, which Gwen gathered so she might share the same words of encouragement, hope, and inspiration that God used to sustain her spirit throughout her life.

Life throws many situations our way: victory, defeat, joy, disappointment, happiness, and hardship. These encouraging poems cover the different twists and turns of life and will enlighten, support, and teach all who read this inspirational book.

It is Gwen's prayer that all who read this book will be edified and will draw strength to continue to live and pursue God. This book will serve as a reminder that God will never leave you or forsake you. God will always speak to you, no matter what you're facing or going through in life. As you read the poems, meditate on the words and allow the Holy Spirit to comfort, encourage, and inspire you.

Made in the USA
Lexington, KY
19 January 2013